DENTAL IMAGE
BRANDING

HOW TO
Create Optimal Patient Impact

Janice Hurley

INDIE BOOKS
INTERNATIONAL

ISBN-10: 1-947480-62-6

ISBN-13: 978-1-947480-62-9

Library of Congress Control Number: 2019938156

Designed by Joni McPherson, mcphersongraphics.com

INDIE BOOKS INTERNATIONAL, INC.
2424 VISTA WAY, SUITE 316
OCEANSIDE, CA 92054

www.indiebooksintl.com

CONTENTS

FOREWORD

In the last eighteen years, Janice Hurley has implemented systems that have transformed my office from Walmart to Nordstrom.

She is always current with fresh ideas and plans to help my office succeed in this exciting profession.

Last week during a second consultation, one of my patients commented how nice it was that my team spoke the same language. He was impressed with how we presented treatment, the comfortable atmosphere, and the level of care given to each patient. He said, "You must be working with an expert in the field."

"That expert is Janice Hurley," I was proud to say. If you want someone who will help you achieve your goals and transform your office into one that sets you apart, then look no further than the wisdom in this book. Thank you, Janice.

Jeff Berger, DDS
Sonora, California

PART 1

WHY DENTAL IMAGE MATTERS

❶

Why You Are Losing Patients (Hint: It's Not Your Clinical Skills)

Ever been handed a worn, torn twenty? You know, that twenty-dollar bill that has seen better days? It's limp, wrinkled, and a bit dirty. Set that same twenty next to a brand-new, crisp twenty, and you'll be drawn to the new twenty every time.

Offer both twenty-dollar bills to a friend and see which one is the winner. New and crisp always prevails.

The same thing happens at work every day with our patients. They are drawn toward individuals who exude personal self-confidence and pride, those who are pressed and polished and look like they are happy to be at work. When they enter an office, people want to be able to tell at first glance that the team members value themselves and the patients they are ready to serve.

Understanding how others experience you is important because it affects how others treat you, which ends up affecting how you feel about yourself. Seriously, your self-esteem changes based on the feedback you get from others and the mental messages you give yourself. It can and will fluctuate daily, if not hourly, depending on circumstances.

Joseph De Loux, a neurologist and author of *Your Synopsis Self*, documented the daily fluctuations in our self-esteem based on the information our brain assembles. We notice how others treat us, and confidence and perception of our worthiness vacillates.

Do you know people in the dental industry who have this problem? They face eroding profitability because they focus too much on attracting new patients and not enough on patient retention by building trust.

From my experience as a dental practice management consultant with a successful twenty-five-year track record,

I give dental practices clarity by showing them how to remove common practice financial frustrations that they have total control to fix. To spread this message, I wrote this book.

You Are Being Judged

This book is for everyone at the dental practice, whether you work in the administration of the practice or in the clinical aspect. The advice I offer is for the dentist, hygienist, office manager, and dental assistants. It takes a village to create an image and a consistent practice brand.

Sometimes a group photo with three or four team members communicates that personalized dental experience.

Consciously or subconsciously, people make judgments regarding whether your dental office is to be trusted and whether you *look the part* of competent professionals. Two important adjectives to add to your list of image goals would be *well-groomed* and *successful*. These are not goals for vanity's sake, but instead for the visual reassurance of patients' encounters with us; they affect the quality of their overall experience.

Think about it: we know packaging matters when we hand out toothbrushes and floss in a nice gift bag with the office logo versus a plain white bag or no bag at all. No one can argue that the toothbrush and floss did not *really* increase in quality or value with the addition of a nice bag, but the pride you felt handing those same items to your patient in the personalized bag is clear. Packaging effects your patient's perception of what they are receiving.

Another important reason to pay attention to your professional image and grooming is the power of the first impression. Understand that every day in your practice you may encounter new patients or their family members for the first time, and that these first impressions are, indeed, lasting ones. Clinical team members, be they the doctor, the hygienist, or dental assistants who take the time to make sure their shoes are spotless—that their lab jacket or scrubs are washed and ironed as well as tailored for fit— communicate to their patient that they value and respect the patient and the practice. Hair should always be worn up and off the shoulders, and minimal jewelry and natural-looking makeup are the best recommendations for anyone working with patients.

The Flowered Wallpaper Syndrome

Sad, but often true, is the fact that the longer we have been in practice and the greater our clinical skills and set of services offered, the more likely we are to no longer look at things from our patient's point of view.

Why is that? I think this occurs for two reasons.

The first reason is that familiarity leads to not seeing things at all. The longer you have been exposed to your reception area, your outdoor signage, or your parking lot, the less you see it. I call it the flowered wallpaper syndrome.

After the kids had graduated from high school and were off to college, my parents moved and purchased a new home. New for them, but thirty years old. When the grown kids visited the new home for Christmas, they all said the same thing: "This is nice, but the flowered wallpaper up on the kitchen ceiling has to go."

My mother's response was quick and clear: "Oh, yes, we're going to replace that right away."

Time went by, and Mom was busy with things other than the wallpaper.

Thirty years later, that wallpaper is still up there on the kitchen ceiling. Her justification? "I don't notice it anymore, so it doesn't bother me."

A second reason we often stop noticing our environment falls on the dentist: the more a dentist gets involved in advanced clinical courses and the use of the latest technology, the more a dentist often stops seeing things from the patient's perspective. Naturally, the dentist now spends a great deal of time focusing on what goes on in the treatment room. Typically, the other aspects of being a practice owner receive less attention.

Of course, the quality of care, efficiency, and team training are crucial. But a practice often loses patients before they ever get back to receive the dentist's care. If the dentist's focus is back there on equipment success rates, new procedures, and services, then the dentist may have *no idea* how much treatment was never done because the practice lost patients on the front end.

See your practice through the eyes of prospective patients. Here are six areas the dentist and the team need to look at *now* if they want to keep valuable patients and attract new ones.

1. **Take a good look at the view of your building and its signage from the street exposure.** Signage needs to be big and clear

on what services you provide. The fact that your patient can receive dental care at that location is more important than your name or the name of your corporation. Signage on your building or in front of your building has to be large enough to be legible from the street, or it is actually worthless. It is important to understand signage limitations and possibilities before signing your initial lease. Negotiations to optimize your exposure should take place before the lease is signed or the decision is made to locate your practice on this property. This marketing aspect is far too important to ignore.

Before choosing a location for your practice be sure you are allowed optimal exposure in your signage. The other business signs next to yours affect your image.

2. **Examine your parking lot, front door, and the walkway up to your door with fresh eyes.** The door needs to have clear signage on it that tells the patient, yes, you have arrived at your intended destination. This signage should not state that you are out for lunch or show your business hours, because that type of communication is out-of-date. Instead, make sure the name of your practice is large and in a current format. Etching on glass is very attractive and current.

3. **Pull out a smartphone and find yourself.** Do what your patients do after they hear about you from friends or coworkers; see what they see and do what you can to look at it with a fresh eye. Gone are the days when your website was a one-and-done project. Instead, it needs to be updated every two to three years. You also always want to look at the mobile version of your website, since over 80 percent of the time that is how your patients are looking to locate you or another dentist in your area. Above all else, it must be quick and easy for your patients to access what matters most to them: your location and your services. Ideally, your patients will see your mobile website displayed the same way they see their phone apps. Dentalfone is on

the cutting edge, providing that initial look for
dental offices, and it's so popular because that's
what patients want: ease of use and clarity. You
truly have to keep up your image from the very
first encounter so they will choose you.

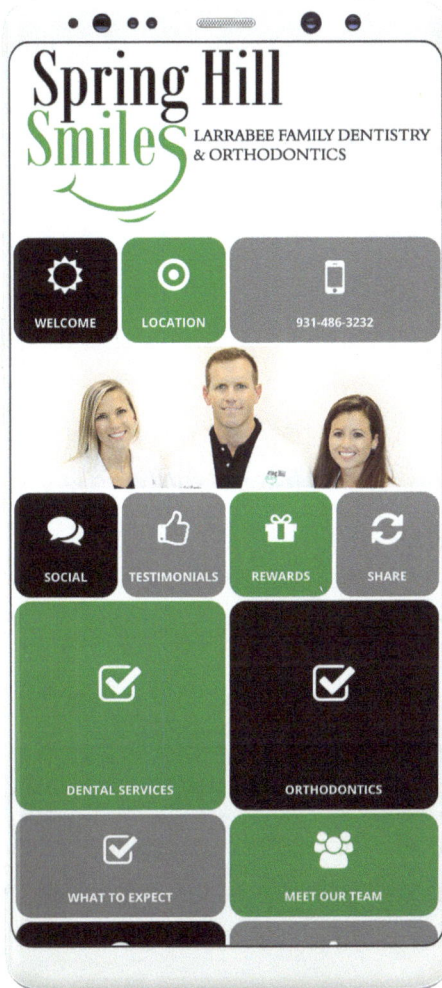

*You want to be branded on mobile applications. That is how people
find you. I recommend using Dentalfone (www.dentalfone.com).*

Video of all kinds on your website and on review websites allows your patients to connect with you more quickly and on a deeper level. Text is being read less and less; videos are seven times as likely to be opened than information to be read. Text continues to be important for search engine optimization, but photos and videos are what your patients react to the most strongly. According to Matt Bowman, owner of Thrive Internet Marketing, "One of the biggest strengths of video marketing is that it's highly visual and auditory, which means it's easier for many users to remember than text-based content. When customers remember your video marketing content, they also remember your brand, which translates to more sales and leads for you. What's more, customers typically like to share videos they enjoy, which can expand your online reach."*

4. **Check out and keep current with your social media footprint.** Anything that your potential patients can find on the internet affects your success, the number of new patients, and the quality of patients that you can count on each month. You might wisely be spending thousands

*Bowman, Matt. "Video Marketing: The Future Of Content Marketing." *Forbes*. April 02, 2018. Accessed August 27, 2018. https://www.forbes.com/sites/forbesagencycouncil/2017/02/03/video-marketing-the-future-of-content-marketing/#13f5b0ff6b53.

*Resist using stock photos on your website or social media posts;
instead, professionally taken patient photos are more impactful.*

of dollars each year on marketing, but are
unaware of what your patients see first. When
your patients enter your name or location into
an online search, they will see results including
review sites such as Healthgrades, Facebook,
and Yelp. These review sites allow you to add
your photo, videos, and practice information
when you claim those sites. There is no charge
for this process, and you will want to make sure
you take the time to populate each site. These
review sites may well be one of the top two first
impressions potential patients see when they look
for you online. Patients are very impressionable
and easily swayed by the quality and number of
your reviews. There is no doubt you have to use

Your social media posts can be fun, showing your playful side as a team.

software that optimizes your patient's postings and check to see that you have responded to their postings, both good and bad. Someone in your office must have this assigned as a priority duty, because reviews will often be your potential patient's initial introduction to you. Make it an office goal to respond within twenty-four hours to a review, whether negative or complimentary.

5. **Call yourself.** By far the most undervalued responsibility in the dental practice is the answering of phones**.** The person that I choose for this crucial responsibility has the best verbal skills in the office; he or she is clear that the person calling is actually more important than the person standing in front of the desk, who is already a patient. The first three seconds of what the person hears from the person answering the phone determines the caller's impression of the practice. Phone calls should be recorded through marketing and patient communication software so that there is no possible excuse not to know exactly what is being said on every call coming into or going out of the practice. The dental software Weave has this ability, as well as Patient Prism. In my opinion, this aspect of patient marketing needs ten times the attention that it gets. It is important that the team members

put in that position know the difference between talking and communicating. The best individuals are the ones who keep in mind the goal of successfully scheduling and screening. Outstanding front-desk team members have high self-esteem and confidence, so they are comfortable in the role of serving others. These people can make or break a practice, and this is where a practice can lose the most patients without even knowing it.

6. **Be sure you have the right message for those on hold and that the phones have different messages on the answering machine or voicemail, depending on the situation.**
   There will always be times when the phones can't be answered as you would like due to team meetings, holidays, or the limitations of your business hours. Make sure the message your callers hear is current. When they do reach the practice, but you have to place them on hold, make sure they hear prerecorded information that places your practice in the best light. You do not want a local radio station with another dental office's ad playing as your patient waits, and you can't just have silence.

When I speak to dentists or business owners, they often want to hear about the biggest dental image mistakes.

While I like to be positive, these are the blunders that do indeed drive away patients. The next chapter will highlight the top mistakes and advice for improving your dental image branding.

2

Top Ten Dental Image Branding Mistakes that Drive Away Patients

Image matters every day. Think consistency, congruency, and complimentary when it comes to your image and brand. Dental professionals who are willing to look at photos or video footage of themselves from patients' perspectives will benefit from that information when they view it with an objective eye.

Take a Really Good Look at How Others See You

Everyone in the practice should ask themselves: "Do I consistently look the part of a confident, up-to-date health professional?"

The first step to improving in this area is to make an honest appraisal. If someone took candid photos of you throughout the day, would your face, your posture, your language, and your grooming show how much you value yourself? Would it all be a positive reflection of you at your very best?

I once met with Mike Yankoski, author of *Homeless in America*, who as a young college graduate purposely put himself in the position of being homeless for five months in six different states. He said one of the more surprising outcomes from this experience was what it did to his self-esteem and his ability to portray a sense of confidence. Because others had treated him with such a lack of respect and in fact predominantly treated him as invisible, he started to subconsciously believe he was. And although those five months constituted less than 2 percent of his life, that time had a substantial impact on how he then projected himself to others after the fact. Sometimes we, too, have participated in less-than-supportive relationships, and it has affected how we perceive ourselves and therefore how we project ourselves.

Sometimes it's not others at all who most frequently speak ill of us; instead, it's our own self-talk that is less than uplifting. John Milton, a seventeenth-century English poet, said, "The mind is its own place, and in itself can make a heaven of Hell or a hell of Heaven." How many times a day are you undermining yourself with negative thoughts like these?

- "I should have done that better."

- "It's so like me to mess that up."

- "Here we go again. I knew I'd run late."

- "I can't stand this job."

- "Nobody listens to me."

- "I hate the way I look."

Our minds, our thoughts, and our self-talk are always on. According to some brain researchers, we have about 60,000 internal thoughts per day. That's one thought per second during every waking hour. The goal isn't to stop the thinking, but to encourage positive, loving thoughts toward yourself. I promise you that the more you truly respect, take care of yourself, and like yourself, then others will follow suit.

I know many of you have had long-term relationships with your current employer and it has either felt like or been referred to as a marriage, right? Through thick and thin, in sickness and in health, full schedule or empty schedule.

Well, like a marriage, there are some crucial steps to falling in love again with each person you work with. A good place to start is examining your expectations.

Your Expectations

Start first with your expectations. I can't tell you the number of times I have heard a team member complain about the personality of another, only for me to reply, "What were you expecting?"

"Well, I was expecting that he (or she) would change," they say.

"Really? Why?" I reply.

The truth is, what you see is what you get when it comes to someone else's strengths and weaknesses. It is good if you can put a magnifying glass on the things you like about each and every person you work with.

We all create unnecessary stress in our lives with our expectations of others. Don't set yourself up for unhappiness, or your coworkers for failure, by expecting them to change. For the most part, they really don't. That doesn't mean you can't clear up misunderstandings or work on needed systems for the office. But if you get stressed over personality traits others had when you were hired, then give yourselves both a break and let it go. All of us only make changes in ourselves, and only when we work on it.

If you are on the practice team, can you make your relationship better with your doctor and others? Of course you can, if you want to and if you work on it. And like a good marriage, it will be worth it.

Teamwork is great, but one more thing is needed: patients. With that in mind, now we turn our attention to the biggest image mistakes that are driving patients away from the practice.

Top Ten Dental Branding Mistakes

Here is my research on dentistry's biggest branding blunders and how to overcome them:

1.   **Not being truly curious.** Do your best to look at your long-standing or new patients with genuine interest regarding what matters to them. Look to see how they are feeling right now, at this moment, while they are in your office.

2. **Not being respectful.** A very beneficial office cultural practice is to make a habit of always being positive and respectful. Never assume you already know what your patients have to say, and resist giving them the same canned answer you've said for twenty years. Remember that what might be old news to you really matters to them. The more frequently you are required to give an answer to the same question, the more likely you are to sound canned and insincere. Take a breath before answering that all-too-familiar question you have heard so often.

3. **Not documenting thoughts and feelings.** Clinical notes should be the most referenced notes in an office, and clear documentation on what your patients said will empower each of you to be effective with that patient. Use quotation marks (" ") whenever possible when

Work together to be sure you standardize where patient notes can easily be referred to in terms of what is most important to the patient, including fears. Nonpatient time should be scheduled for training.

documenting the patient's own words. Those same words repeated back to them will make them feel heard and connected to you. These specific words can be used by the whole team even though the next team member wasn't the original listener.

4. **Not being proactive and protective of your patient's time.** Make sure all vacations, holidays, and courses are scheduled as far ahead as possible on your yearly practice calendar. The doctor's schedule should not be considered more important than the patient's. The doctors can, of course, plan to spend their time any way they choose—and they should. It just needs to be planned a year in advance whenever possible. This is a core leadership issue that cannot be faked one day and then forgotten the next.

5. **Blaming the lab.** Having your patient return for yet another seat appointment because you didn't check the fit on that crown before the patient got in the chair is inconsiderate. I have sat in offices when the patient is in the chair, and we are just now discovering their case is not in, or the wrong restorations were in the box. Digitally scanned impressions now have restorations coming back without a corresponding study model, so checking on the model cannot occur.

Handsfree headsets work wonders in a dental practice so you can make notes while a patient is speaking with you. The newest versions are almost impossible to detect.

6. **Not taking administrative notes seriously.**
Oftentimes, the patients communicate their needs, wants, or desires in person or over the phone to the administrative team. Write those important communications down in the patient's chart or clinical notes if this will impact case acceptance or treatment. I strongly recommend you type your notes while the patient is talking to you so the patient can see that you value input. I suggest saying, "Let me make a note of that for Dr. Berger here in your chart; she will want to know about that." Headsets for administrative team members are a great source of efficiency, and in my opinion should be mandatory.

7. **Favoring tasks over listening.** When your patients are present, ask a question with full eye contact and interest. Every patient that arrives and exits should always be spoken to at eye level. Assistants, hygienists, and doctors should be in front of the patient and speaking with gloves, masks, and eyewear off when communicating. Yes, there is a great deal to get done in a short period of time, but the patient in your chair is paying you right then and right there for your full attention. Patients will believe you spent more time with them when you give sincere eye contact at their level.

8. **Not being informed about your patient's dental and health history.** Make it a Standard Operating Procedure in your practice that you will never re-ask your patients for information they have already given you in one form or another: for example, health history, dental history, or patient information.

9. **Making patients wrong.** I know we would never do this on purpose, but making patients wrong is done quite frequently. We make them wrong every time we correct them; when we inform them that what they thought about their insurance coverage was wrong, for example, or when we let them know we like a different mouth rinse than the one they are using. We can still be a source of information to our patients, but not at the cost of how they feel in our presence. We can agree with what they say and then lead them to additional perspectives on the subject. It might sound something like this. Patient: "I have 100 percent coverage for my cleanings." Team member: "Ok, that's certainly good to know. Your understanding is your cleaning is covered at 100 percent?" Patient: "Yes, it always has been." Our Team: "You're right. When you were receiving a prophy, which was proper treatment for a healthy mouth, your

insurance did have that as a benefit. Because things have changed with your health and periodontal treatment is now needed to address your periodontal disease, their involvement has changed. Your insurance benefits can be used, of course, and let's look at that together."

10. **Forgetting the patient is connected to their teeth.** The patient's self-worth is lowered or raised, depending on how we reference their current dentistry or home care. The worst example I have seen was a patient who was kindly seen by the doctor on a Saturday as a favor to someone they mutually knew. The patient traveled 500 miles to see this well-known cosmetic dentist, as she was heartbroken and without hope with the dentistry that had been done by another provider. The current dental care had left this patient with bulky, unnatural-looking teeth and the loss of tooth #9 from trauma during the preparation of that tooth. The dentist was trying to move the midline and had removed bone. There had been nothing wrong with that tooth previously. The patient arrived into the new practice fairly depressed and frightened that she would always look the way she did upon arrival. The talented, skilled dentist took a look and knew differently. That

was *good news*, but instead of offering her hope and reassurance, he tipped her up and said: "It's crap; it's all crap." Was he accurate? Yes, he was. But what would have been better received would have been, "You're going to be fine. I am so glad you're here. We can fix this for you." Many times, when it comes to telling the truth, we can either omit it completely or alter the way it is phrased to benefit how our patients experience the news.

My Journey into Dental Image Branding

Before I lead you on a guided tour of how to improve your dental image branding, I should share the path I have taken to be able to offer this advice. Mine was a circuitous trip into the world of dentistry and image.

I unexpectedly became a single parent when my children were six, four, three, and two years of age. Although I had a college education, I had not worked outside the home while I was married. I soon learned that I needed a job. Not just any job, but a job that would give those four children a college education and straight, white teeth.

I figured if they had those two aspects going for them, they could get jobs and buy their own cars, so the pressure would be off me to buy them. I did what anyone does who needs employment: I put together a resume and picked out something to wear for the interview.

The clothes I wore were from my lifestyle at that time. I had clothes to go work out at the gym or clothes to go out on a date. At those job interviews, I was not successful. As I knocked on doors and tried to find employment, people were quickly judging my qualifications based on the way I was dressed.

With those outfits, I could get a date, but I couldn't get a job. And I needed a very serious job.

Because employers' responses to me were consistent, I knew it was something I was projecting and something I needed to fix. Taking responsibility to change, I attended a course for women on professional image in Visalia, California, and I immediately learned what I was doing wrong. I was thirty-four years of age, and I looked young and attractive, but I certainly didn't look professional or capable of earning the income I needed to earn.

So, I went to the local JCPenney department store and bought a boring brown suit for $37. I knew it was boring because my six-year-old daughter Jennifer said it was. Armed with sheer determination, I knocked on doors again, and the response was different.

I was initially hired as the health educator at Woodlake Family Health Center and then eventually promoted to executive director. Because of the recognized success I had in this field, I was hired to consult with rural hospitals on physician retention and practice management. I taught such business principles as scheduling, time management, healthy overhead criteria, standard operating treatment procedures marketing, and the like. After two years of consulting in the medical arena, a company called Practice Perfect recruited me into dentistry, and the rest is history. I fell in love with dentistry.

Twenty-five years later, I am known as a dentistry image expert. In presenting my programs on practice management systems at the major dental meetings and study clubs, I spoke about the importance of verbal skills, body language, and showed before and after photos of professional office attire.

People who work with me say I am clear and direct. They understand that I work for the health of the practice, because everyone wins. I am willing to say that how unattractive bathrooms look matter, and that chewing gum might alienate a patient, along with the doctor checking his cell phone in front of a patient. I am always willing to talk about the hard subjects from the patients' point of view in service to the health of the practice. I understand that it's hard to see ourselves and our environment if we have been in it for some time. I believe we all have a common goal, whether we work in the administration of the practice or the clinical aspect: we want to provide our very best. Sometimes we just need an outside set of eyes to help.

Working on site with a team guarantees that your consultant will work with the actual challenges your team faces and challenges can be resolved.

As time passed, I started to get requests to speak specifically on the subject of professional image in dentistry.

As one of dentistry's foremost image consultants, I am a personal coach on how to best use what you have available to achieve success. I serve as someone who can help you see yourself, your team, and your office as others now see you.

An image consultant listens to how you say you want to be perceived and then lets you know what you are doing now to effectively communicate that objective and what else you're *not* doing yet that you could do to enhance your presence. It is often hard for those in a dental practice to see themselves as others see them. That is because we can't stand back and feel the energy that we are exuding, and we often don't have a fresh, unbiased eye about our strengths and weaknesses.

Let's put it in terms of what dentists do every day, which is diagnose and then recommend treatment. I do that same thing. I listen to how you want your professional brand to stand out and where you want to be within the dental arena. I provide fresh eyes on the videos and photos used on your website and social media. I help dental teams understand how their external presence is essential to a healthy practice.

When it comes to perception, patients use their five senses: sight, hearing, smell, taste, and touch. Part II of this book examines how your image is shaped by the sensory messages your practice is sending out, and how to improve that from a patient's perspective. Yes, it is all about what they see, hear, smell, taste, and feel.

PART 2

HOW TO OPTIMIZE PATIENT IMPACT

❸

Improve What the Patient Sees

Are you familiar with this adage? "If we want to really understand someone's situation, we need to walk a mile in their shoes (or moccasins or sneakers)." I think we can apply this philosophy to our patients' everyday experiences in the dental practice.

My suggestion is to take a look from the patient's viewpoint and see what they see from their perspective. Look high and low. Look all around. See the dental practice as they see the dental practice. A first question is, where to start?

Try Looking Up

My recommendation is to start by looking up. On the high side, when your patients are tipped back in their chair, and they are looking up, what do they see?

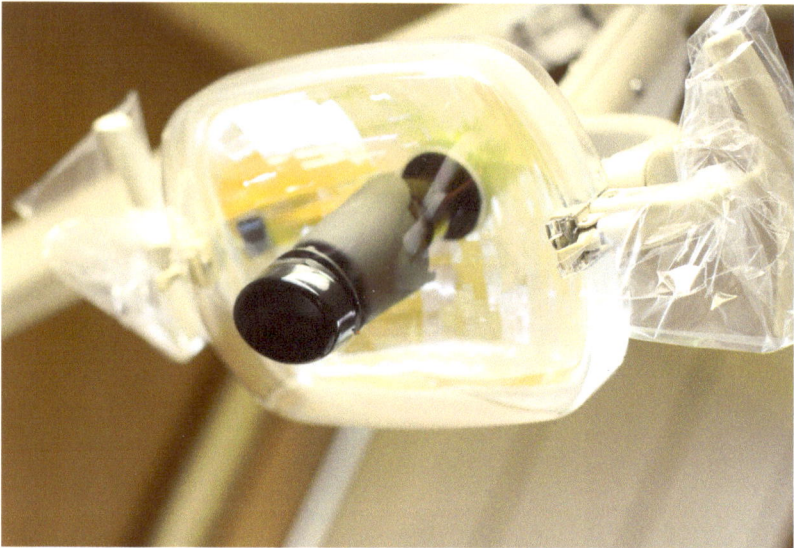

Many times we no longer see from the angle that our patients are looking. The condition of your light and their glasses are often missed.

Before the light is shining in their eyes, patients are seeing something. What is that something? Is it:

- Old posters of cartoon characters

- Leaky ceiling tiles

- Twirling teeth on a mobile

- Chipped ceiling paint

- Old television screens

Also, please double-check the cleanliness of:

- Your own glasses or loupes

- The overhead light

Your patients are so very close to you that impeccable grooming is always a plus.

- The protective glasses you hand your patients (no scratches, please)

A simple but impactful marketing tool is to have your patient's name up on your computer screen right in front of them so the can see "Welcome Stephanie" or if it is a returning patient "Welcome back Stephanie." We do this for every patient in every room. For offices that do not have a monitor in front of the patient we have an attractive white board that is changed for each patient.

Now Look Down

After you look up, next, look down. Do you like what you see, and is it clean?

Your patients will notice the carpet and the base of your chairs on their first visits into the office when their senses are heightened. Anything worn must be replaced.

Finding a service to properly clean and maintain the physical properties of your dental practice can be a challenge. Frequently, when it's time to cut overhead, a practice will look at reducing what is spent on cleaning services. There is certainly no guarantee that spending more gets you more, but sometimes it does. Either way, it's important to keep your eyes open from the patient's perspective. Often it is the bases of your chairs that get missed in the cleaning process. Sometimes it's a carpet that has seen better days and can appear unclean and out-of-date.

Then Look Around

Now that you have looked up and then down, look around. How would you describe the overall esthetics of your treatment rooms? Do you have equipment that stands out as being dated? Do you have dental chairs or x-ray heads that creak and groan when you move them?

Patients are looking down and around, and sometimes they take notice of things we take for granted. Countertops should not be used for display or storage. The mind sees clutter when items are shown horizontally. Take the same items and store them vertically. Please take a look at your treatment room with the eyes of a first-time patient who is noticing the environment with keen alertness.

Time for a Surprise Inspection

Since we know that people's perception is their reality and your patients form strong impressions from visuals, take a minute to do a six-step team inspection of your own.

STEP ONE. *Right now, this minute, take a team picture.* Take one head-to-toe of each individual team member so you can see what your patients will now see for the day. Looking good for the yearly team picture isn't as important as how you show up every day. Take random pictures of one another and see what you think for yourselves. A dress code should be listed in all personnel manuals and given to new employees upon hire. Decide

Purchasing matching shirts can be a positive aspect in your office branding. These shirts can be worn outside the office for team events.

you want to bring the very best of you, visually, verbally, and energetically, every day. It is a personal choice that will pay off. We really do feel better when we look better. The limiting factor is often simply effort.

STEP TWO. *Check out your nails.* Clinical team members should have nails no longer than one-eighth of an inch, with neutral nail polish, and please, no acrylics. Administrative team members can wear their nails a tad longer, as long as they, too, are manicured and polished. A dark or neutral nail polish is preferable to bright pastels or pinks and orange nail colors. Gel manicures are helpful, as they last longer than a traditional manicure. Male team members should have little to no nail showing, and cuticles

One of the most important things is that others see us with smiles on our faces.

and skin should be trimmed and moisturized. We really do notice other's hands more than we notice our own.

STEP THREE. *Survey the shoes.* Are your shoes clean and appropriate for your best professional presence? Check out the backs of your shoes for wear marks, and check out the toes for scuffs or missing leather. Look at the soles to make sure they aren't tired and tawdry. Your patients look at your shoes more often than you do, I guarantee it.

STEP FOUR. *Check the hair, please.* And this time, I am talking about ear, nose, and facial hair. It appears that as we age, our hair just grows in different places. Men need to wax, cut, and tweeze ear hairs, and women need to clip nose hairs and wax or shave facial hair as they get older. Look, I know no one wants to talk about it (except those patients of yours who are up close and personal and have to look at it). In our business, it should be a daily must to groom before we go to work. Avoid showing unappreciated chest hair. Men, if you wear a V-neck scrub, wear a T-shirt under your scrub top.

STEP FIVE. *Look to see if pressed and polished.* In honor of your patients, do you look as great as possible every day? Are scrubs crisp and clean? Do team members have name tags clearly displayed on their right side, just below the collarbone? (Name tags worn on the right side are easier for your patients to read as you introduce yourself and shake their hands; we tend to put them on the left side when we are right-handed.)

STEP SIX. *Examine these dos and don'ts.* Do all clinical team members have their hair up and away from their face and shoulders? Do the men in the practice have all facial hair trimmed tightly and the back of their necks newly shaven? Waiting to have the back of your neck shaved until you have your six-week haircut is waiting too long. Beards work well when clearly taken care of and when your patient base also appreciates them.

Shoes and Good Service

Step three above talked about shoes. Let's go deeper on that subject.

As a dental professional, I think we are often amazed at how our patients are seemingly unaware of how their teeth look. What seems pretty obvious to us goes unnoticed or unvalued by patients. The same can be said about dental professionals and their shoes.

Neither teeth nor shoes should be dirty, worn out, or ill-fitting. Everyone would agree in principle to this fact, but often our shoes are a sad representation of our dental team. No dental practice has clean shoes written up specifically in the mission statement, but if you care about what patients see, you will pay attention to your shoes.

Often our shoes are the last item we put on and something to which we never give a second thought. Our patients, on the other hand, do indeed see our shoes. So, whether you are a chairside assistant, hygienist, or a dentist, the patient will look at your shoes far more closely than you look at your own when they are in your presence. Patients' senses are heightened when they are in the clinical rooms, and they are looking for cleanliness and work-appropriate attire. Patients who are brand new to the practice will weigh the overall cleanliness of your appearance, shoes included, with more importance on the first appointment than at any other time.

Important above all else, of course, when it comes to shoes is fit; comfort first and foremost. Most appropriate work shoes will require an investment of $100 or more, with support and comfort being the most important criteria.

Take this quick test to see how you and your shoes measure up:

1. Are they work-appropriate?

2. Are they spotlessly clean?

3. If they are leather, are they polished?

4. Are the heels in good shape with no obvious wear?

5. Is the back of the right shoe, typically your driving heel, unscuffed?

6. Are the toes clean and undamaged?

7. Do they look fairly new and current?

Take just five seconds to look at your shoes from a brand-new perspective. Look to see what others would see if they were looking at your shoes and making a connection between them and the quality and cleanliness of the dentistry they would receive (as if there were indeed a direct correlation).

Some shoes will require that you give them a little attention, some will require a lot. Others might need to be retired permanently. Setting a high standard for yourself allows you to, with good conscience, know you are bringing your patients your best.

A Final Thought about Clothes

Your style and the clothes you choose reflect and affect your mood, health, and overall confidence. Scientists call this phenomenon "enclothed cognition." Adam Hajo and Adam D. Galinsky, both professors at the Kellogg School of Management at Northwestern University, write in the July 2012 *Journal of Experimental Social Psychology* that enclothed cognition "involves the co-occurrence of two independent factors—the symbolic meaning of the clothes and the physical experience of wearing them."

These researchers had subjects perform tests while wearing a lab coat, like medical doctors wear, a coat like painters wear, and not wearing either coat. They found that subjects' sustained attention increased while wearing the doctors' coats in a way that their attention did not increase while wearing the painters' coats or no coats.

In Part III in this book, we will examine clothes in more detail in a chapter about dress codes for a dental practice. Now let us turn our attention to what a patient hears that affects the image of a dental practice.

4

Improve What the Patient Hears

There is no doubt your patients are affected by the sound within your dental practice. We, on the other hand, often become immune to the noise level.

Patients' senses are heightened in your practice because of possible anxiety and certainly there's an increase in what they hear because they are guests in your domain. It's a good idea, therefore, to pay extra attention to keeping disturbing noises to a minimum. Some examples of areas of transgression are:

- Snapping your gloves off too close to the patient's face

- Dropping instruments loudly onto the tray

- Yelling down the hall when something or someone is needed

- Loud noises from machinery in the lab that is too close to patient treatment areas

- Cell phone alerts of any kind (something that seems ridiculous to need to mention, but it still happens, sadly enough)

Here is some more sound advice to improve your dental image pertaining to noise.

Noise Between Dental Rooms

The optimal treatment room setup has privacy in mind. Open-bay treatment areas, often used in orthodontic or pediatric practices, leave little to no possibility for privacy. Choosing a more private setup for other specialties is strongly encouraged.

If operating in an open-bay environment, pay special attention to those times you will need privacy and use of a separate consultation room. If you have separate treatment areas, be mindful of how noise travels. The more you have rooms that can be closed off with a door or sound screens, the better.

Patients do not appreciate hearing others' conversations in the next room; neither do you want them to have to experience dental sounds that raise their anxiety. Sound control can be challenging, but something worth your consideration, whether you are just starting in the design of your practice or you are looking at your existing treatment room configuration. Some of my clients have used sliding screens between rooms to muffle office noises.

Noise Control Starts at the Reception Area

The energy and atmosphere of your reception area makes a strong impression on your patients. Most offices have wisely equipped the entry area so music can be played. The best source of office music is Pandora, Spotify or another premium music application that avoids commercials.

The last thing you want is patients irritated by having to listen to stress-inducing commercials for used cars or bail bonds. I have been in a dental practice that did not have uninterrupted music in the reception area, so the patients, unfortunately, were listening to commercials from a competitive dentist in the area.

Sitting down at eye level to talk about appointments and finances increases the opportunity for confidentiality.

Music in the reception area might reflect your practice brand or the music popular with your patient base. Be mindful of both the music and the volume of the music where patients are waiting. Music played at the right volume will help muffle conversations taking place up by the administrative area. I strongly recommend that you sit out in the reception area during a regular patient day to hear what they hear. Avoid subjecting your patients to conversations with other patients over the phone about outstanding treatment or payments. Those conversations, when possible, should not be heard by other patients.

Music on Hold

I suggest using a service that lets your patients listen to your prerecorded message while on hold. Again, you do not want your patients hearing a local radio station. Instead, patients on hold should be hearing about the wonderful services you offer and your willingness to offer them the type of appointment they need as quickly and conveniently as possible. The background music to your message on hold can be wisely chosen by you to be aligned with your practice brand.

Headsets for Your Patients during Treatment

Quality headsets are a wonderful way to set your practice apart from others, creating a soothing, considerate patient experience. The sound of the drill is no one's

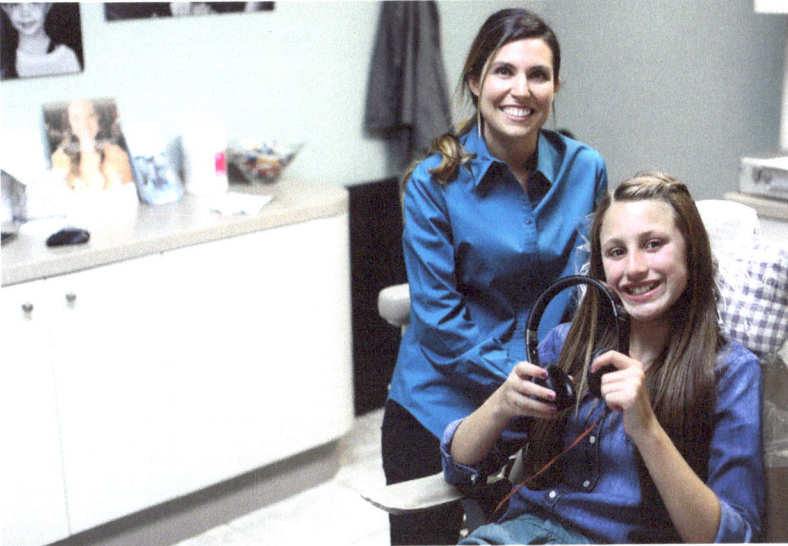

Quality headsets are a must to improve your patient's experience.
Having their music of choice ready for them is a customer service plus.

favorite, and you can't count on your patients bringing in their smartphone with their own headset or earbuds. Their own equipment also won't be as good at blocking out other sounds.

Music changes the chemistry within your patient's body and brain, therefore changing their thoughts about returning to the dentist. Having a comfort menu that each patient fills out before treatment including music preferences allows you as a practice to have their music all ready for them (please see the comfort menu example in the appendix). The beauty of Pandora and other streaming services that allow you to play specific genres and artists on demand is that we no longer have to buy a wide selection of CDs for our patients to choose from.

Positive Conversations

Positive conversations make patients feel better about their experience in the office. I recommend that all conversations be directed to patients themselves and that the team does not have negative conversations while patients are being worked on.

Your saying to your patient throughout treatment "Good job" and "You're doing great" plants in their mind the fact that things are indeed going well. This practice is grounded in the fact that we believe what we hear; if you are forever

Offering the option of NuCalm and other calming agents is respectful and sets you apart from other offices that might ignore patient anxiety.

asking a patient "Are you all right?" it heightens the sense that they need to be on watch for pain or discomfort.

Having a left-hand policy in place with your practice, wherein patients have been instructed by the hygienist or assistant to raise their left hand if they want you to stop for a second to speak, is a great idea. This lets you and the patient know you expect things to go smoothly and a shared goal is that you will finish as quickly as possible. Always let the patient know before starting about how long the work will take and how smoothly you expect things to proceed with outstanding results.

Let your patients hear how much you delight in serving them. Yes the operative word is delight. Every office should offer a new patient tour that is clearly scripted to present the benefits of each area of the office shown. When you do so resist asking the patient if they would like a tour but instead say: "I am so glad you're here. Let me give you a quick tour of the office to welcome you."

At the end of their appointment instead of asking if they would like a warm towel go ahead and place it on a serving tray and let them know it often feels good at this point to wash their face and hands. Be sure to take the patient's bib off as soon as possible and only place it at the last minute as needed to truly protect their clothing.

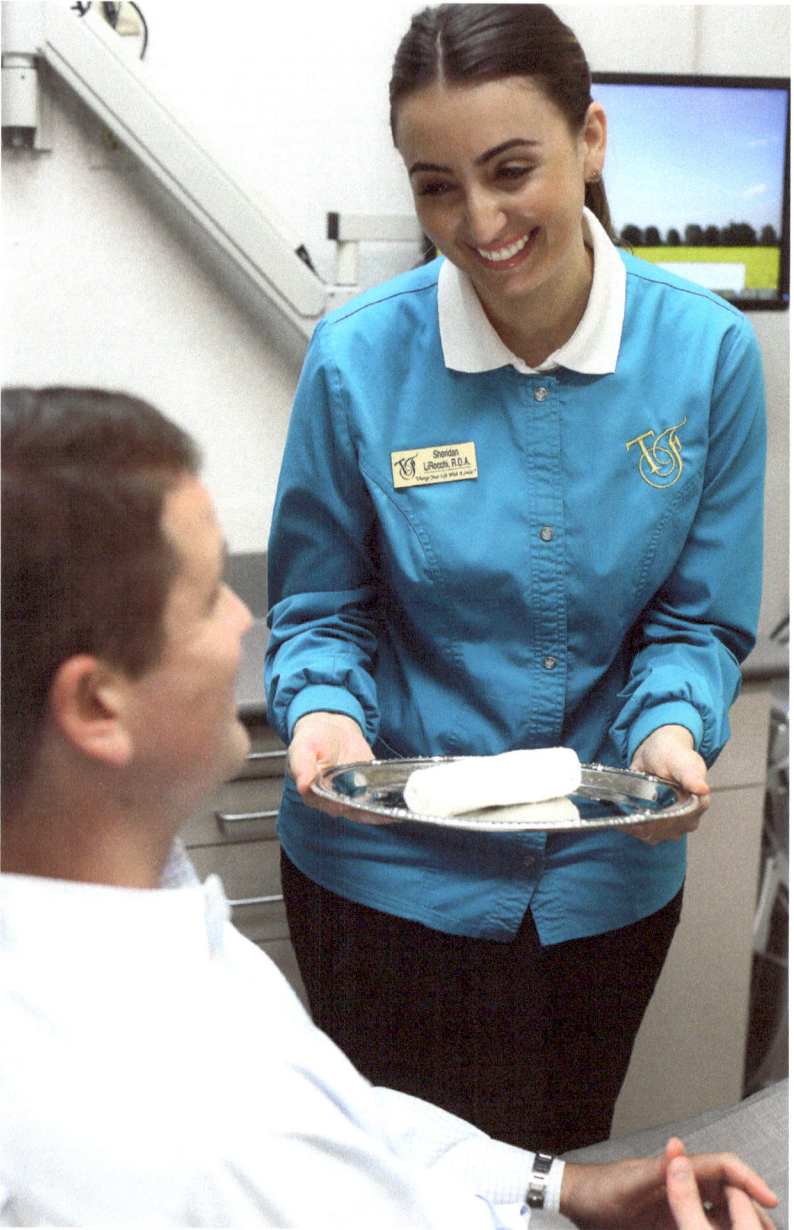

Warm scented towels given at the end of every appointment set you apart with minimal cost or effort.

Let Them Hear You Care

The new patient call. One way to stand out in your practice is to pleasantly surprise your patients by having the doctor make new patient phone calls. This marketing tool is so effective in promoting your brand as caring and personable because the call does indeed come from the doctor.

Offices implement this system by giving their doctor a list of patients who will be new to the practice either for an office visit or a comprehensive exam. The list has the day of the appointment, the patient's contact information and type of appointment. We don't list the reason for the appointment because we're not going to discuss that over the phone. The doctor usually gets this list at the end of the week and makes these calls at his or her convenience.

Suggested script: *"Hi, this is Dr. Wiltz, your new dentist. I wanted to call and let you know I am looking forward to seeing you next Thursday at 8 a.m. for your comprehensive exam. If you have any questions before then please let Ms. Rosalyn know by calling the office; otherwise, I will see you then."*

Sometimes the patients do pick up the phone and they are always very flattered that you would call. Offices that implement this marketing system greatly reduce their no-show rate and have made a favorable impression right from the beginning. This marketing practice absolutely works wonders.

Care calls. These calls are made for all patients that have received treatment that involved anesthesia or a visit that the patient might have found difficult in any way. Patients who receive an appliance should receive a care call whether it is for sleep apnea or for whitening their teeth. The call is to show you care and to hear any necessary feedback.

Care calls are optimally made by the clinician who assisted at that appointment or the hygienist. Care calls are made a day or two after the impactful appointment.

Suggested script: *"Hi, this is Ebony from Dr. Wiltz's office. How are you doing today?" Then continue with, "I just wanted you to know that everything went really well yesterday at your appointment. You were a terrific patient and we're excited about the results. I know I gave you written homecare instructions, and I wanted to see if you were able to rinse as suggested when you got home."*

The intent of the call is to show you care and to reassure the patient that things went well. It is not to show concern, so we don't say: "Are you all right?" Go back over any homecare instructions if you have given them and document in the patient notes that you made the call. Be sure to write in the patient's own words anything they had to say on this call.

A smile is by far the most professional greeting your patients look forward to when they arrive. Keeping our focus on them and not ourselves is always the goal.

When your team embraces the importance of these calls to the health of your practice, and you understand how impactful they are in patient retention and attracting new patients, you'll carve out time in the day to make these happen. These calls are just as productive as yet another patient in the hygiene chair.

5

Improve What the Patient Smells

The sense of smell has the strongest effect on your perception of someone or someplace. The only thing stronger than the visual experience is what you smell (or more importantly, what your patient smells). This information, coupled with the reminder that your nose adjusts to smells they are continuously exposed to, should alert you to the importance of smell within your practice.

How many smells your patient is exposed to depends on products you use and the location of your lab in proximity to your treatment areas. But no matter what the scenario, be sure to remember the olfactory impact.

What might some of the culprits be?

Eugenol used to be a standard in the dental practice. A liquid used to calm a sensitive tooth, when mixed with the powder zinc oxide, it created a particularly difficult smell to get out of the office and one that conjures up many a bad experience for patients from childhood.

Drilling on a tooth can bring up both the smell of the enamel and the dentin. Teeth with decay or teeth that receive root canal treatment will also, of course, present odors from the result of bacteria.

Many patients do not like the smell of Lysol used as a cleaning product because they associate that with the smell of hospitals or nursing homes.

Here are some other unpopular office smells patients tell us about:

- Orange solvent
- Denture cleaner
- Denture reline material
- Infection of any kind
- Fluoride varnish
- Food cooked in the team lounge

In addition, there are these team transgressions:

- Perfume
- Cigarette smoke
- Body odor
- Bad breath from food or periodontal disease

What to do when patients mention unpleasant odors? Believe they exist, empathize with what your patients are experiencing, and take it to heart. *Fix it!*

You want to fix the offensive odors in your practice in three ways.

1. **Use essential oils.** Essential oils and similar aromatic products should be used and alternated regularly. Diffusers in the reception area and throughout the office are a gift to both you and the patients. Suggested fragrances are spearmint, orange or lemon. I am not a fan of synthetic smells used in candles, such as the smell of popcorn or cookie dough; the verdict is out for me on whether the smell of fresh baked goods or popcorn is something I want to smell if I am a patient.

2. **Preview the odor.** Nobody likes surprises. When you know there is going to be an odor, tell your patient ahead of time what to expect. Even go so far in your graciousness to apologize. Example: "Mrs. Turner, I want to let you know, so there aren't any surprises, there is likely to be a bad smell when we remove your bridge. That's from the decay below the crown that has had a field day in that moist environment. The good news is, once we remove the decay and design

your new crown, you won't experience that. You're one of our favorite patients, and I just wanted you to know what to expect."

3. **Make sure your policy and procedure manuals address team hygiene.** I know this should go without saying, but personal hygiene is paramount given the proximity with which each person works with patients. Patients tell us they dislike the smell of cigarettes, perfume, body odor, or general bad breath. All of that seems forthright and easy enough to understand. What is not as easy is addressing this challenge with an individual team member. But address it you must. I find it is helpful to ask a new team member reading the office guidelines just how they want to be addressed should an issue arise. Most inevitably say they want to be told as soon as possible and told privately. I make a note on their employment agreement that this is how they wish to handle communication regarding hygiene issues. Because the employees were allowed to choose how they wanted something to be dealt with, it helps later should the need arise.

6

Improve What the Patient Tastes

One of the best ways to understand your patients' experience is to be a patient yourself. There is nothing like experiencing dentistry firsthand to understand what taste might be a negative experience for them and then doing everything you can to avoid it.

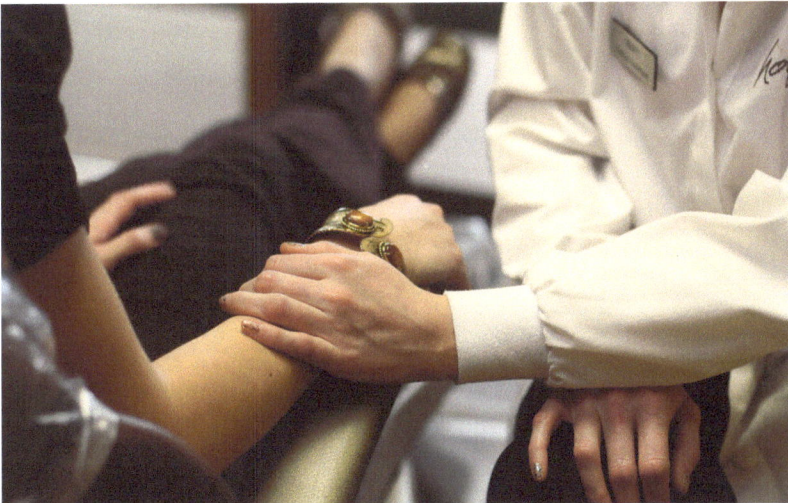

Make a connection with your patient when you are letting them know you expect things to go very well and that you are there if needed.

How something tastes and flavor preferences are certainly individual, but some recognized products we use in dentistry today are considered universally distasteful. There are three systems you want to have in place in order to improve your patients' dental experience with you.

1. **Acknowledge as a team that you use products that have a less-than-favorable flavor.** Here is a partial list:

   - Material used to make temporary crowns

   - Anesthetic—lidocaine is the worst

   - Etchant material

   - Varnish

   - Bonding agents

   - Impregum

   - Denture reline material

2. **Critical to your patients' experience is telling them what to expect.** As a team, you have identified or experienced those less-than-optimal flavors, and in fairness to patients, you want to tell them ahead of time. Your patient will appreciate your thoughtfulness when you reduce the element of surprise. Better to say, "There is a bitter taste with the anesthesia. I just wanted you to know that it will

be there, but very briefly, as I do everything I can to suction it from your mouth."

3. **Do be on alert, as the dental assistant or hygienist, to suction or rinse out bad-tasting product as soon as you can.** There are so many things for you to think about as you deliver dentistry, but staying on top of keeping your patient comfortable should be a priority. Please know that your job is to be continuously rinsing to make your patient comfortable. There is no need to ask the patient if they want their mouth rinsed out, as many of us will say, "no thanks," just because patients don't want to be a bother.

Being aware and sensitive to what your patient is physically experiencing requires ongoing focus to be with your patient. Pay attention if you find your mind wandering elsewhere as you go through routine tasks. We all strive to be our very best, and remaining conscientious about this aspect of your patients' experience is very thoughtful. Being an excellent provider for our patients is a privilege. Living in the moment with your patient is time well spent. When we let our minds wander to the past we can't change or project out to the future, we lose the opportunity to give excellent customer service.

7

Improve What the Patient Feels

This chapter is a bit of a departure from the previous six. The time has come to examine what patients feel; not just in the sense of physical touch, but what they are experiencing emotionally.

There are numerous opportunities to let your patients feel good about themselves. Sometimes these opportunities to make them feel good actually arise from not doing something you might have normally done previously that unknowingly made them uncomfortable.

Here are three tried-and-true rules about making others comfortable in your presence.

1. **Delight in their presence and have it register as soon as you see or hear them.**

   How you feel about your patients will register for them within the first second after you see them. A warm smile as soon as you see them walk into

A delighted welcoming smile is always well received.

the door or up to your counter will let them know you are indeed delighted to see them. Let the word delight be your grounding point for the affection you wish your patients to feel.

A common mistake when patients call our offices is to sound chipper with a greeting and then disappointed when you hear who has called, or what they are asking for. I know this for a fact to be true in even the most patient-oriented offices because I listen to their recorded calls. Take some time to listen to your own. It's critical to quickly respond in a positive manner to whatever request your patient might have with a statement such as, "I would be glad to do that," or "Absolutely."

Resist talking over patients as though they were not there when you are in treatment rooms. Unless your patients have music playing through top-notch headphones, they can hear what you are saying; the focus should be 100 percent on them.

2. **Recognize that patients are attached to their teeth, and anything you say about their teeth can feel personal.**

There are so many times we need to reference a patient's teeth and the problems therein. Knowing that to be the case, we want to be acutely aware of how sensitive patients might be to bad news.

Hearing negative things about their teeth or dentistry performed by previous dentists creates the strong chance of being taken as personal criticism. So, keeping that in mind, tread carefully and with purpose. Your goal is to communicate the problems that exist and what will happen if they do nothing, but also to leave them whole as a person. How do we do that?

You want to be sure to make plenty of positive references before you deliver the bad news, and it's wise to use permission statements when appropriate. Here are a couple of suggestions for tough situations.

Example: For patients who have a lot of work in their mouths, including some that has broken down and much that needs to be restored, give them a compliment or two first and then use a permission statement:

"You obviously value your teeth. It's clear you have invested both time and money in your dental health. You are to be commended. If it's OK with you, may I share the current condition of your teeth?"

Example: For patients who rated their current dental health very high and also said that their dental health was very important, but after you look at the X-rays and do your exam, you see things differently:

"Maria, I read that on a scale of one to ten, you rate the importance of your dental health a ten, would that be correct? And that in terms of the health of your mouth, right now you rated yourself a nine. Clearly, you place great value on the health of your teeth and gums, and that's wonderful. Based on the information that I have from your exam, may I share what indeed is healthy in your mouth and point out any areas of concern?"

Example: When you're ready to show a patient areas of decay, failing restorations, and other challenges, be sure to take the opportunity to point out when previous treatment was done well and compliment that restoration:

"These two crowns that you are looking at right here are in good shape and are ready to keep that tooth healthy for a time. The crown in front of those two has served you well, but it is no longer protecting your tooth. In fact, because it has pulled away from your tooth and there is a space open for food to be trapped in that area, we know the decay is progressing quickly."

3. **Remember the important things a patient says.** Make sure it is written down. Don't re-ask

questions you should as a team already know, and secondly, refer to what they previously had said was important. I know this system of not re-asking the patient a question they have already answered seems glaringly obvious, but I see it happen all day long in every office I visit. The only way to avoid this is to have three systems in place:

- **System One.** Every team member needs to know what has been asked on all of the patient's paperwork and know where to find the answers previously provided by the patient on that paperwork.

- **System Two.** A phone slip must be used by the team member taking the initial phone call, and the hygienist or dental assistant should be given this phone slip to reference what has already been said.

  Examples: "Rashele tells me that your wife encouraged you to make an appointment with Dr. Jeff."

  "Rashele tells me that you have sensitivity on one of your molars on the lower left and that it is keeping you awake at night, even with the use of Tylenol."

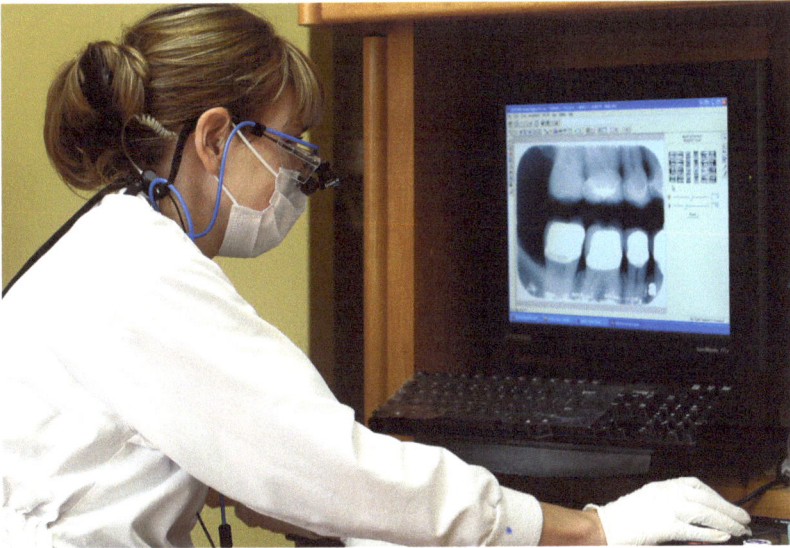

Standardizing note taking and documentation is both efficient and a practice builder. Morning huddles can be used to give positive reinforcement for excellent documentation.

- **System Three.** Each team member must know where to find the information listed for the patient's initial chief complaint. You want to designate a specific place to put this critical information for easy access. You can't count on rereading all your clinical notes to find the initial motivator. You must also as a team know where referral information is located, and the progress made. Your patients think you know about them; show them you do. Doing so puts them at ease and increases their perception of trust and confidence. When people trust us, they move forward with our recommendations.

Many offices have found that it works well to create a "flag" for the patient's main motivation, so that it pops up on the schedule. A patient's motivation for treatment or cause for hesitation to receive treatment is key and often does not change throughout their time in your practice.

PART 3

WHAT COMES AFTER THE FIVE SENSES

8

Implementing a Dress Code

Determining a dress code for yourself and your team is as important a business decision as choosing your office signage, which insurance plans to accept, and which CE courses you will take. It's true because it affects your bottom line.

The top two reasons to clearly determine your office dress code and enforce it are:

Reason 1. New patients are determining within the blink of an eye if they have chosen wisely when they selected your office. This quick determination is based on their emotional response when they meet you and the team for the first time

Reason 2. Studies show that our personal actions are affected by how we are dressed. And how we are dressed changes how people treat us. Every day, we are encouraging our patients to trust us and follow our clinical

Dr Jeff Berger from Sonora California did not have a dress code in place when he first started his practice but he could see the benefits of implementing one to increase the level of professionalism.

recommendations. When our patients see us in the very best light and treat us with respect, it encourages us to treat ourselves and our recommendations with confidence.

The best place to start with a dress code is at the beginning—the beginning of the practice and the beginning of each team member's employment. Dress codes should be formalized in writing and included as a part of the office personnel manual, with each potential hire offered a chance to read the policies before accepting employment. The dress code should outline all of your clothing and personal care expectations in detail.

Dr. Jeff today in Sonora, CA. The clinical team has a specific uniform from head to toe that is provided by the practice. The administrative team has a clothing allowance to ensure consistency.

Create Guidelines for Hair, Makeup, Jewelry, Shoes, Uniforms, Body Art, and Perfume

Include photos in the manual to show the optimal way to wear a uniform. We use photos for training on tray setups; the same technique works well for being clear regarding professional attire.

The biggest mistake that doctors make is either to think that their team members' professional appearance will never be a problem or to lead from a position of weakness— afraid that their team members will be upset with them if they are told specifically what is acceptable and what is not. My experience in this area is just the opposite. Having extremely specific dress code guidelines and enforcing them consistently leads to team pride and reduces the internal friction that occurs when everyone is left to make these important business decisions on their own.

I once worked with an office that had very specific attire guidelines, and the team and the doctor were almost always in compliance. That's why it was so unusual when one of the chairside assistants showed up in colorful high-top tennis shoes—something very different from what was in the office manual for shoe requirements. Further discovery uncovered the fact that this assistant was actually just looking for attention—any attention—from her dentist. Her dentist had recently hired a new assistant with expanded functions, and the dentist couldn't stop raving about how wonderful it was to have this new team member on board. In this incident, the dress code violation wasn't about lack of clarity on the policy, but one of no longer feeling valued by her employer. Sometimes when a problem involves people, it involves complicated emotions, but they are worth pursuing.

As a leader in the office, you will know just how well you are doing when you see how you respond to a team member's complaint about a breach in your policy. Check first to see that everything is clearly stated in writing, and then use your next team meeting to bring up the fact that perhaps you have not been as clear as you should have been about your expectations. Address the rules, not the individuals, if your policies and enforcement have been lax. If you have excelled in this area, bring the team member with the dress code violation into your office and address it clearly and quickly. I suggest that repercussions for breaches be outlined in the employee handbook as well. The goal is to be as clear as possible from the beginning, with little to no need for these conversations.

Sustaining an Optimal Image Culture

Let's discuss orchestrating your patients' first impressions.

When patients view each team member of your practice as polished and professional, they are more likely to trust you, accept your treatment advice, continue care with you, and refer their friends.

You probably already recognize this fact, but do you know how to create an optimal dress code and how to implement yours with the clarity and consistency needed to make it successful?

As I consult with individual practices to help team members design their most effective personal presence, I find that nine principles apply every time.

1. **Be willing to put it in writing.** In my work as a dental image consultant, I frequently observe that

if your practice does not have a written dress code, or it is not complete or well considered, situations will arise: you will have to tell others what to wear and how to wear it, and that will be stressful for everyone concerned. Maybe you have already experienced the embarrassment of trying to enforce an unwritten rule of which someone might simply have just been unaware.

A written dress code covering attire and grooming is a gift to yourself and to your team. If you haven't already created yours, this will be a relief to you and to everyone. Written guidelines prevent confusion and misunderstandings, and help each team member feel confident and appreciated.

2. **Include the administrative team.** Administrative team members should wear professional attire. That usually means that men should wear dress shirts, dress slacks, and ties, and women should wear a jacket, blazer, or sweater (in a solid color or small pattern) over a dress or a blouse with a skirt, or dress slacks. There is certainly a need to take into account the prevailing norms of your location and the attire of that community, but after twenty-five years of consulting daily in real world dental practices, I see over and over again that the smiles on team members' faces show approachability, and proper attire shows respect for yourself and your

patients. Over and over again, I see the benefits of dressing so others see you in the best light; let your facial expressions and body language show how delighted you are to see your patients.

Many times a cardigan sweater can evoke just the right level of professionalism and be flattering for most team members.

If you have more than one administrative team member, allow them to choose their own styles and colors. Your goal is to have the team feel as well-turned-out and professional as possible, and they will not feel that way if they have to match, because they will not all look great in the same outfit.

Each administrative team member should wear comfortable, professional, closed-toed shoes. While they might not be on their feet as often as the clinical team, comfort is still vital to creating that comfortable and welcoming atmosphere for your practice.

3. **Decide what your clinical team members will wear.** I am excited about the number of uniform options we enjoy today. Be sure to choose quality materials and properly fitted attire in colors that harmonize with your office's color scheme. I am partial to lab jackets for the entire clinical team, worn over crisp shirts or blouses with pointed collars and nice cotton pants.

    Avoid large, V-necked, traditional scrubs. They are usually inexpensive and made of poor-quality material, as well. Dentistry no longer has to settle for these items, although they are still used for prisoner attire. Please, no scrubs with flowers, teeth, or animals, no matter what type of dentistry you practice.

    I am really not a fan of golf shirts as office uniforms. They are not flattering and are too casual for the optimal dental environment. It is also hard to keep them crisp and clean; after several washings, they lose shape and color.

    Remember to specify colors for clinical team shirts, pants, and shoes. Be just as detailed in specifying the color of nail polish and socks to be worn.

I do not favor color days, where specific colors are worn for each day of the week. It is more expensive for team members to designate so many uniform colors, and it creates opportunities for error.

4. **Mention everything, head to toe.** Your dress code should include your expectations for makeup, jewelry, hair, nails, and daily grooming. Your patients see you and your team members up close and personal, and they tend to notice every detail. It might be awkward to talk about this, but in our business, daily grooming is vital. It is better to include something in your dress code that seems obvious to you than to assume any unwritten rules are understood.

5. **Subsidize the attire you want.** It is a good business practice to pay for the look that supports your practice brand. By doing this, you honor the team that puts great effort into looking professional every day, and you contribute to team loyalty. In addition to buying any uniforms that you require, I recommend that you provide administrative team members with a clothing allowance.

An appropriate amount might be $500 per person two or three times per year. This outlay is listed as an employee expense and included when measuring employee overhead.

6. **Introduce expectations at each job interview.** Allow prospective team members time to read the dress code, ask questions, and confirm that they are willing to dress according to your guidelines every day.

7. **Make spot checks fun.** Have team members take photos of one another frequently and randomly. Looking good for the yearly team picture isn't as important as looking professional every day.

8. **Include photos in performance reviews.** Celebrate and reward consistent professional appearance. Patients notice this aspect of your practice, and it is a vital factor supporting your own success, so be sure to acknowledge and appreciate this accomplishment.

9. **Live it yourself.** A dress code is more than one section of a personnel manual; it defines a way of life, demonstrating professionalism and respect. I encourage you to lead by example. You can personally commit to bringing the very best you to work—visually, verbally and energetically—every day. It is a personal choice that will pay off.

And in Summary

After twenty-five years as a dental image consultant, I can say with complete confidence that business owners can avoid a great deal of turmoil and time by writing out every detail that is important to them and then paying attention to compliance. A sample dress code outline can be found on my website: http://www.janicehurley.com.

And now, let's conclude with my most important image advice: Be happy.

As in all aspects of your practice's success the consistency of the leadership plays out each day, and the team takes the doctor's lead.

9

Happiness Is A Choice and a Big Part of Your Office Image

If you're happy and you know it clap your hands (clap clap)

Many of us grew up on that little song, which encouraged us to let our faces show just how happy we were. The consequences were that, if we indeed expressed out loud that we were happy, it would show on our faces.

So besides grade school children clapping and singing, who would you say is happy? And are *you* happy? Some of us would say that depends, and some of us would identify ourselves quickly as happy people. Thinking about your patients, couldn't you pretty much place them in two groups—happy and not happy? The interesting fact is that happiness, for the most part, is not dependent on our ever-changing situation. You're either happy or you're not for the majority of your life, because happiness is a mindset.

We can tell when we are around someone that is genuinely happy with themselves and happy to be with us.

Well, then, what is happiness dependent on? Studies tell us that it is 50 percent genetic—written right there in your genes, whether you look on the bright side of things or whether it comes more naturally to you to be a bit down or experience anxiety or even depression. Your parents didn't just give you the coloring in your skin and eyes. Your DNA programming also affects how you view the world.

The big surprise is that only 10 percent of our happiness is situational—dependent on what is happening to you. We can all have a strong, momentary positive or negative response when, let's say, we lose our job, or our baseball team makes it to the finals, etc., but after those initial reactions to extreme situations, our overall happiness meter just moves 10 percent one way or the other. So, how happy you were *before* you got the job of your dreams determines just how happy you'll be once you have the job of your dreams. How happy you are when you see your favorite patients on the schedule for a productive morning is roughly how happy you'll be when you don't have your favorite patients on the schedule for the afternoon.

The Seven Deadly Image Sins

As a summary of what robs a practice of happiness, I want to cover some image sins. As I visit dental practices around the country, some common transgressions occur again and again. I call these the *Seven Deadly Image Sins*:

1. **Running Late.** Anything more than ten minutes indicates real lack of respect and system problems within your practice. This has to get top billing on your to-do list.

Introducing yourself to each of your patients is a gift and an opportunity to thank them for coming on time.

2. **Visible cell phones, whether up at the front or with the clinical team.** When patients see them, even when they are turned off or turned over, it lets them know you don't have your full focus on them.

3. **Describing a patient's present dental condition in negative terms.** Remember patients are connected to their teeth. When you describe their teeth in a negative manner, you make them feel bad about themselves personally.

4. **Not making a big deal out of every new patient.** You can do this by greeting them as soon as they arrive, by name, and giving them a new patient tour.

5. **Changing your patients' appointments.** When you cancel or move your patients, it shows disregard for their time, and they are more likely to move their reappointed appointments with you.

6. **Old, tired, worn-out equipment and more.** This may include anything from chairs, reception area furniture, and less-than-pristine restrooms.

7. **Keeping your patients waiting too long once they get back to the treatment area.** No excuse for running later because you are inefficiently delivering treatment or overbooking.

What dental office is without sin? No office is perfect, and that being said, the dental office should work together as a team to avoid these sins.

It's a funny thing, the whole idea of teamwork and getting along, isn't it?

Working together means experiencing the ultimate in synergy and productivity for the good of the practice. It sounds like something from a glossy brochure, right? But we should all agree that an optimal goal is to really enjoy one another.

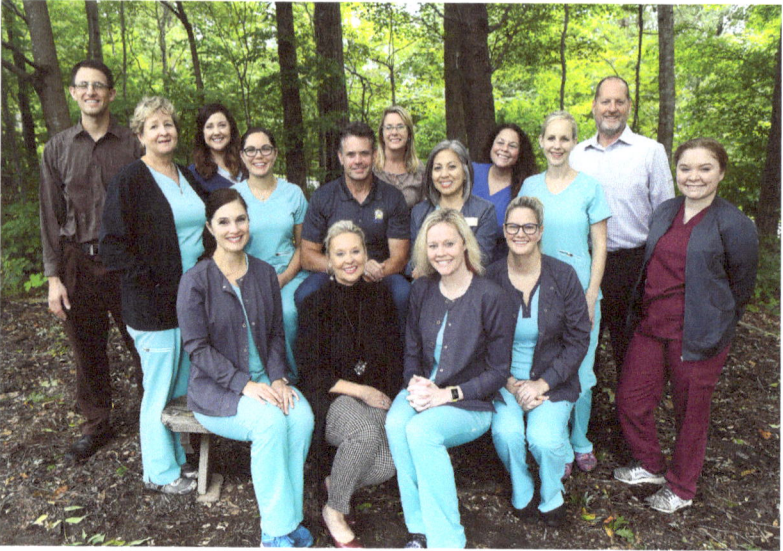

Each team member brings his or her own special personality and skill to the practice. Celebrating our diversity is important.

If, as a dental practice team, you have ever struggled with teamwork, you're not alone. Harmony and teamwork sound so great in principle, but we often find ourselves at odds with others. There are some interesting things to recognize when team members contemplate what it takes to really enjoy one another and to enjoy those with whom we work.

Let's address the relationship between the team and the doctor or doctors. If you are a team member, I hope the relationship with the doctor is everything you ever wanted in a professional relationship. If so, I would venture to guess that you knew a lot about what was important to you in choosing your current place of employment and sought that out (or you got really lucky, right?). Or perhaps you're the type of person who really knows how to get along with others, and you've made your relationship with your doctor work for both of you.

Either way, this is what I see in a great relationship between every team member involved. You are going to have a doctor or two to work with daily. What would help you as a team member, whether clinical or administrative, get along with your employer?

Think Respect

When it comes to getting along, I think about the late, great Aretha Franklin, who sang about "R-E-S-P-E-C-T, find out what it means to me."

Respect is, in my opinion, the number one piece needed in a great relationship between doctor and coworkers. So, ask yourself, right now, on a scale of one to ten (ten being the highest) how much do you respect your doctor? How much do you respect each member of your team? How much does he or she respect you? Be honest. Both aspects are crucial.

I am a firm believer in the fact that we train others how to treat us. So, if you gave yourself less than a ten in terms of how much respect your doctor or someone else has for you, let's work on that. Here are some probing questions to consider:

1. Do you walk and talk and look like you respect yourself?

2. Are you comfortable holding eye contact when both listening and speaking?

3. Do you know for sure the things that are really important to your other team members in terms of work ethic and expectations? Have you been given those expectations in writing in an employee agreement?

4. Do you have the clinical, administrative and/or communication skills *that others admire*?

5. Are you up to date and excited about the areas of dentistry your doctor is interested in?

6. Do you speak up in a constructive manner when you have an opinion about policies and procedures for the office?

7. Are you viewed as upbeat and positive by others you work with?

If *any* of those might use a little improvement, please get clear on what you need to do.

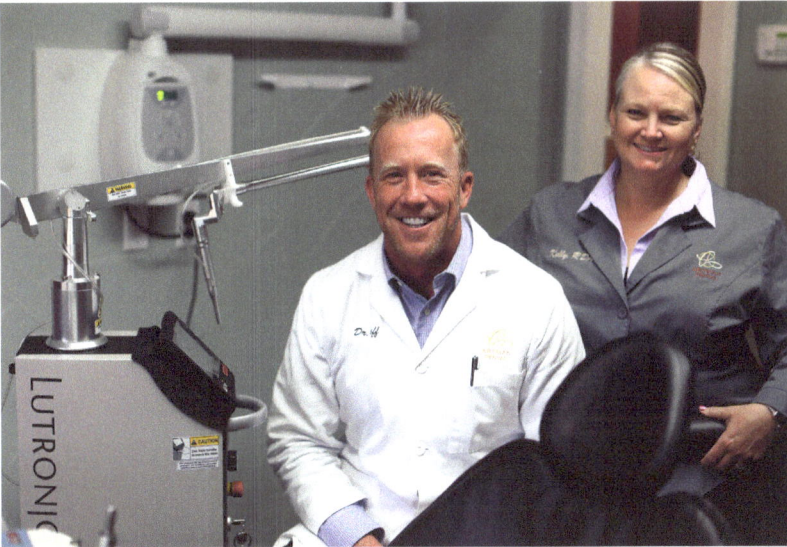

Our patients are drawn towards our confidence in both our clinical skills and our personal presence. Confidence is a gift we give ourselves and others.

judgment that we had chosen the wrong office could have been avoided with more office training. What contributed to her deciding she was not in qualified hands? The assistant with whom she had spent time kept apologizing throughout the taking of impressions, photos, and X-rays, saying: "I am sorry, I haven't had much training in this; I am really new here."

I convinced my friend to stay with our office selection by reassuring her that this was certainly a one-time anomaly and that the highly recommended orthodontist was sure to supervise her case and therefore affect her outcome. There is a happy ending to this story—my friend got excellent care and results, and she has long ago forgotten her first impression. But clearly, I have not—and did not recommend others to that office.

Adequate training *before* team members are required to spend time with a patient is crucial to the professional image of the office. I have often known offices to get new equipment, new software, and commit to new in-office systems without taking the time to train. That's what we all need in order to learn a new skill: time.

We all learn differently and at a different pace, but the majority of us prefer to embark on learning without the added pressure of a patient in place. In truth, all of us learn better when we are not nervous and when we have enough time to practice the same thing over and over again. Repetition is the friend of all learning, and the newer the skill, the more important it becomes to give yourself permission to practice again and again. Whether it's sanctioned team time or time you spend on your own before or after scheduled patient care, it's in your best interest to give yourself permission to learn in your own way and at your own pace.

Avoiding a less-than-optimal impression can sometimes mean you have to speak up to your office manager or doctor regarding your need for more training. It can also mean that, while you are learning, you don't let your patient know you aren't completely comfortable with what you are doing. My friend wasn't uncomfortable with the technique of the new assistant, but instead, she became more and more alarmed as the assistant's well-intended apologies made my friend aware of her lack of expertise.

Patients want to know they are in good hands and have chosen the right office, so my recommendation is that you keep the fact that you are new or inexperienced in a particular technique or skill to yourself. "Fake it until you make it" or "ignorance is bliss" are mottos that can both apply.

Another recommendation is to be sure that the person training is a good trainer, not just someone who is the most knowledgeable on the skill, because those can be two different areas of expertise. Haven't we all been trained on new software or a new camera by the expert in the office who takes it for granted we already know more than we do? I know I have. If the goal is to project the most professional image possible, then getting enough training and the right training should be an office priority.

Until then, speak up. Also, practice until maybe *you* will be the office expert. Why not? We all started from the beginning at one time, didn't we?

I wish you success on your dental image branding journey.

Always remember that patient experience is the key to optimize the financial health of your practice.

Patients want to feel as though you know what you're doing so be sure to practice new skills until you can do them with ease.

Appendix

Patient Comfort Menu

CREATURE COMFORTS

If at any time during your treatment, any of these items would make your visit more comfortable, please let us know.

- **Lip Balm**
  Soothing balm should you experience dryness

- **Moist, lemon-scented towelettes and minty mouthwash**
  To freshen and cleanse and to remove all traces of us from your mind

- **Hand Lotion**
  Healing lotion for dry hands

- **Water**
  Ice-cold bottled water just for you, or room temperature, if preferred

To make your visit a little warmer and cozier, we offer:

- **Blankets**
  Soft and cozy

- **Neck Pillows**
  Supportive and warm

- **Full-body Massage Pads**
  Soothing waves of relaxation

- **Bite Cushions**
  Soft, cushion pillows for your teeth that help relax your jaw when your mouth must be opened for long periods of time.

Coming Attractions

Major Distractions!

- **Music**
  We have state-of-the-art headsets for your listening pleasure. Just let us know your preferred channel of choice on Pandora

- **Movies**
  Let our virtual-reality DVD movie glasses take you into another world, or simply relax and watch your favorite flick on our overhead TV screen. Choose from our wide selection of current movie titles, or feel free to bring your favorite.

  - Comedy
  - Children's
  - Adventure/Suspense
  - Drama

   – Romance

   – Relaxation

To calm the anxious patient or fearful child, we offer:
(Additional Charges Apply)

- **Nitrous Oxide** (Laughing Gas)
A light, relaxing gas which allows you to be fully
conscious and capable of driving after treatment.

- **Sleep Dentistry** (Oral Medication)
A light sleep which can make fearful dental visits
a thing of the past—with no needles

About the Author

A noted authority on treatment presentation and the effective use of photos and video in the dental practice, Janice consults and coaches hands-on and through published articles and presented programs. Even dental hygiene schools use her written protocol standards for both image and effective communication. She teaches at Midwestern University College of Dental Medicine.

After earning her degree in organizational behavior from The University of San Francisco, Janice has invested more than twenty-five years as a dental consultant, helping her clients gain higher treatment acceptance and attract higher-quality patients. As an international author and speaker on what it takes to project professional excellence and confidence so others feel it instantly, her goal is for everyone to use professional energy for personal success. She is wildly enthusiastic and supportive in helping each office find its own stand-alone brand. Celebrating one's uniqueness while serving the needs of others is a treasured gift.

Janice's energy is contagious. Her audiences come away as fans, ready to reenergize their lives and their practices. Janice has been a featured speaker with the Thomas P. Hinman Dental Meetings, Yankee Dental Congress, American Academy of Cosmetic Dentists, American Association of Endodontists, Philips Sonicare, Academy of Dental CPAs, Henry Schein, and many, many more.

Attendees of her courses have described her as articulate, charismatic, and powerfully entertaining. She is the expert on personal presence and professional success in dentistry today. Her input on how patients see you *today* is spot-on and priceless. She takes offices through a thirty-point image evaluation that allows those offices to set themselves apart from their competition.

Learn more about Janice and her work at http://www.DentistrysImageExpert.com.

www.ingramcontent.com/pod-product-compliance
Lightning Source LLC
Chambersburg PA
CBHW041118210326
41518CB00031B/142